Doc
Makes Friends

Written by:
Pam Lather

Illustrated by:
Anna Welsh

This book is dedicated to the

children and animals

who are in search of

a forever home.

Doc

This book is based on the true story of "Doc", a 1600 pound Belgian draft horse who moved from the Outer Banks of the Carolina Coast to the Blue Ridge Mountains of Western North Carolina to improve his breathing.

Pam, Doc and Anna

Doc found his forever home at Southern Sun Farm Sanctuary. His first book is titled, "Doc Moves to the Mountains".

Doc is a big horse with a big personality and a big heart. He is kind, gentle and very mischievous!

****

ISBN # 978-0-578-37871-8

About the Author:

Pam and her husband, Ken, retired to the Ashe County,
North Carolina area from Ohio. They both volunteer at
Southern Sun Farm Sanctuary.
Professionally, Pam was a court reporter for over 40 years
working in the court system. She became an advocate for the
plight of abused and neglected children in finding a forever home.
She loves Doc and his antics as well as the mission of
Southern Sun Farm Sanctuary.
Creating a children's book about them both was a new challenge,
while keeping the focus on finding safe, forever homes for
children and animals.

About the Illustrator:

Anna was a Pre-K, K and first grade public schoolteacher
for 18 years. After teaching, she opened
The Blue House Art Studio for children and adults
to have a creative space to use art as an expressive outlet.
She has always loved reading children's books to her students and is
thrilled to be able to be a part of sharing
Doc's story through his book!

For us, it seemed only natural to continue to tell his story!

My name is Doc.
I moved from the Outer Banks of North
Carolina and found my forever home at

In the Blue Ridge Mountains.

It is a beautiful place to call home.
I have made a lot of new friends here.

We are all taken care of by our best friend, Miss Ann.

Spike, the cat, always watches.

The two dogs, Amos and Luke always ride along.

She feeds us hay and oats and apples!
Red apples are my favorite!

9

There are lots of horses,
a donkey, ponies, cats, dogs, and chickens that
live here with me.
Some of us have trouble seeing, walking or
were all by ourselves until we moved here.
Now we are all friends.

Chief was the first horse that lived on the Farm
with Miss Ann.

He likes to give kisses!

When I go to bed at night there is Pango, the pony, Molly Mae, the donkey, and chickens.

The chickens sleep in my stall with me.

Miss Ann tucks us all in and I get a bedtime snack.

An apple!

One week, the chicken, Rita, decided to lay
her eggs in my hay,
right beside my apples.
I did not eat the hay or the apples.

I did not want to break her eggs!

There are children that like to visit.
I love children.

I always seem to be their leader!

Little Leighton read my first book to me,
"Doc Moves to the Mountains".
Reading is very important she said.
She showed me all the pictures.

When she went to leave it was raining.
I kept her dry while she
gave me a hug.

That's what friends do.
They take care of each other.

Little Pango can only see out of one eye.
She is very old and has trouble walking.

One winter day, the rain turned to snow and
the wind began to blow. I wrapped my head
around her back and kept pushing her to go.
She needed to get to the barn.

We both got inside where it was warm and dry.
There was lots of hay to eat.

And she likes red apples, too!

Molly Mae, the donkey, has only three
legs that work.
But she can run really, really, fast.
Faster than I can run.

She follows me wherever I go
around the Farm.

Amos and Luke are the two dogs that
live on the Farm.
Amos likes to play with rocks.
Luke likes to play with balls.

I only like apples!

There are a lot of horses and ponies that found their forever home here at

Southern Sun Farm Sanctuary.

Belle. Duke. Chance.
Rocky. Lady. Dusty. Little Shane.
Ginnie. Feather. Montana.
Kat. Big Boy. Dunny.
Chief. Pango. Molly Mae.

And, of course, ME!

We all hang out together.

There was a fundraiser for the Farm
where they were selling my first book
"Doc Moves to the Mountains".

I was trying to be helpful
but I did keep my eye on that basket of apples!

I was also in my first Christmas parade.
There were a lot of people that came to see me
and, of course, Santa Claus!
It was a lot of fun for everyone.

All my new friends
and I love living in the Blue Ridge Mountains
of North Carolina.

And all of them are learning to
like apples just as much as I do!

Thank you, Miss Ann, the volunteers and
everyone for making

Our forever home!

Yum! Apples!

Discussion Questions

1. What is Doc's favorite food?

2. Who are Doc's best friends?

3. What is his favorite color?

4. Did Doc meet Santa Claus?

5. Can Doc read?

6. What is Doc's favorite game?

7. Can Molly Mae run fast?

8. How does Doc protect his friends?

Southern Sun Farm Sanctuary

Southern Sun Farm Sanctuary rescues abandoned, abused, neglected and unwanted horses, ponies and donkeys.

It was founded and is directed by Ann and John Lisk. Together, their animal welfare experience spans over 50 years. They are known to take the animals least likely to find a home anywhere else. Some will be adopted into loving forever homes while others will live out their lives at the Sanctuary, their forever home, where they are cared for and cherished.

"Saving One Horse won't change the World ...
but it will surely change the World for that One Horse."

To learn more about the Sanctuary or order books, go to: SouthernSunFarm.com / or find us on Facebook

Proceeds from the sale of this book benefit SSFS
which is a 501(c)(3) non-profit organization.

Thank you to:

My husband, Ken, for his support.

Anna Welsh for her illustrations.

Ann & John Lisk for their dedication to
Southern Sun Farm Sanctuary.

And, of course,
to Doc for his huge personality!

Pam

Will there be more adventures of Doc?

9 780578 378718